Brocading
the Verse

For my husband Graham

and my children Melanie and Richard,
and grandchildren Florence, Jessica and Llewelyn

Crumps Barn Studio
No.2 The Waterloo, Cirencester GL7 2PZ
www.crumpsbarnstudio.co.uk

Copyright © Julie Wiltshire 2023

Cover design by Lorna Gray

Printed in the UK by Severn, Gloucester on responsibly sourced paper

CARBON NEUTRAL

FSC
www.fsc.org

MIX
Paper from
responsible sources
FSC® C022174

ISBN 978-1-915067-27-2

JULIE WILTSHIRE

Brocading the Verse

Collected Poems

Crumps Barn Studio

AN UNKINDNESS OF RAVENS

Black acrobats like blindness fall,
tumbling, fumbling, cursing call,
and watch with the eye at the back of their head,
and gather by the murdered dead.
With ruinous hearts the stone-wallers
gorge on victims' fleshy bones.

My addict stamps on dense skull bone,
and wanton sees my spirits fall.
With lifeless eyes and stony
stare, *prruk* my carrion calls.
You peck, peck, peck a soul that's dead,
and pack with wars my withered head.

Cloaked wizards with charred spikey heads,
cast their spells on scavenged bones.
With Bowie knife beaks they hunt the dead,
and circling cleave their fall.
Hell's undertakers croak their calls,
of discourse over earth's hearthstones.

With roving eyes that chill the stone,
the miners shake their sooty heads.
Frosty owls with faithful calls,
fluff and puff their bone-
pale breasts, whilst the moon's smile falls
away they hoot to the long sleep of the dead.

A bearded darkling drops its cloak upon the living dead,
wrapping up sad faces shattered by life's stone.
Dance my harbinger of doom, feast on my freefall,
I try to flee but find your tracks are thorns within my head.
I scuttle like a mouse to shield my snow bough bones,
from east to west I search for peace before my raven calls.

The unkindness of the ravens, hear their tuneless calls,
in the spilling of the seconds before the day lies dead.
The wind whips up a long-felt rage rattling like a bone,
and wipes away the tears I cry that cannot crack my stone.
Caustic are your comments sealed inwards in my head.
You pleasure in my pain so you will not catch my fall.

I will just BE not fall, when my sinful raven calls.
The full moon in my head casts no shadows on the dead.
I am not your stepping stone. Fly free my spirit
        from the bone.

MY WETLAND WORLD

Mellow veil on melancholy vale, ghostly phantoms linger,
fondling mists, softly kiss, the Severn's snaking fingers.
Shuddering woven sultry reeds spike the sobbing rays,
wide mouthed poaching putchers lay, submerged in
      sullied clay.

Whispering trees shed russet leaves, Old Spots on the
      Pippin munch.
Snuffling spicule hedgehogs shuffle, feeding on fattened
      slugs crunch.
Webbed, warts and wefts, jewelled hung, silken spun,
wrapped in hope, cobwebs of dreams, drying in
      the dying of the sun.

A shallow flighted cuckoo beneath the bower,
      clocks the fading hour.
Bewick's swans unzip the Wetlands with their
      pinions of power.
Squawking sinister satanic crows scar the lowlands'
      dripping face.
The mantle of cream pustule homes, on the
      Cotswold's brow embrace.

Amongst gathered harvests in quietude, watchful
      chew the cow and doe.
Weary hedgerows, heavy hung, hold dew-soaked
      berries and inky sloes.
Fairy tale Tudor castles soar and cast their shadows
      on the ley.
Clandestine towers peep half hidden, in the
      snuffing out of day.

Brindled, blurred amongst the mist, swiftly ebbs
      the Severn tide,
Run pheasant run, my rustic sun, over flooded fields,
      nowhere to hide.
A joyful tear leaves its mark upon my dust pale face.
God has plucked my stony heart, and in this wetland
      world has placed.

EXPOSURE

He exposed his lies.
Although his lips cracked a smile,
His eyes showed winter.

INSOMNIA

When the night chews up the day,
And the stars, like the pricks of my consciousness,
Hang weighty above my head,
I PRAY

Whoever is out there hear my plea,
Give to me the sweetest dreams.
Supine, I seek the sleep.
And search for peace.

Each night I regurgitate,
Trenchant remarks,
That sailed in storms my way,
And anchored their scars in the cold light of day.

Tired with night's grave thoughts,
An insomniac suffers in her womb of darkness,
Frozen within the white shroud of sheets,
Awaiting the intensity of day.

Sleep, sleep, count the sheep,
Count to three.
The lids droop, but where's the key?
To stop the mind from wandering.

Like a restless runnel,
I rattle over the cold pebbles of my past.
As memories flow backwards and forwards,
I reach for my pen and sigh.

MORDANT ECHOES

My snatched dreams haunt and taunt me,
As I transverse the tracks of time.
Memories levy a mortmain upon me.
I awake once again cold and shivering,
Wondering if I will ever know the meaning of love?
I cannot mouth the words,
Your wanton ears long to hear.
My lips are pursed and willing to kiss,
But that is all.
I uncurl and stretch my limbs,
And rub my false smiles into your wounds.
You sink deeply into my frayed eyes,
Attempting to unravel the truth,
You cling to my nebulous replies,
With a vice-like grip,
When you ask if I love you.
Hope glues you to this empty vessel,
But still my unspoken words,
Rattle endlessly around my mouth, and sour.
I really want to remain in your arms,
Alas, my love I cannot give, I know not how.
My childhood, my gethsemane,
Where love was snuffed out,
Is my weeping wound.
I still needily grasp at any stray hug.
Alas, I remain the wanton child I was.

A vacuum exists between our two seeking minds,
Where we cannot connect.
Your doubt is a passion that circles the Heavens.
Is there no end to our misery?
Words of no good, just trouble,
To survive them I hid in my bubble.
Transpersonal psychology, will I understand?
Travelling from my deepest wounds,
To the most transcendent capacity of my consciousness.
Alas my love cannot be demanded.
Maybe it is a gift I can tenderly give,
if I push through the pain,
And silence the mordant echoes,
Of the matriarch's cavil and stinging voice.

CANCER THE CRAB
(KNOW THYSELF)

In the blue-green dominion of the sea,
That rises and falls, KNOW THYSELF.
In the powerful ebb and flow of tides,
and the manic ticking of time,
where the world's madness still exists,
a little crab in the fourth house,
born on the cusp,
hides within herself.
In a crusted armour of pretence,
afraid to display her sensitivity,
she fears the unforeseen barbs of rebuff.
A crab called Cancer scuttles sideways,
retreating into the ruins of the deep,
searching for an escape route from life.
She attempts to bury her head in the sand,
allowing no one to spy her vulnerability,
bubbling below the surface.
The timorous creature, the nurturer,
finds solace in her homely shell.
In her flame dipped crust she dwells,
along with ghostly wrecks of the damned.
With cracking claws, the cardinal water sign,
fishes for the fine wine of passion's essence.
Tenaciously she grasps tightly to her dreams,

as the curtain of day hastens to a close.
The silvery moon rises upon its daughter,
and determines her destiny.
In the intermittent sea mist of her flirtation,
she prays for the acquaintance of love.
Between pensive moods and briny tears,
in sand strewn devil damned caverns,
of her mind's perturbances,
intense emotions ride bareback,
amongst the crashing and dashing of waves.

Alas too sensitive for this world,
THIS crab smashes herself endlessly,
against the jagged rocks of rejection,
and shatters.

COBWEB

Filigree spun, suspended, hung,
in autumn's morning mist.
Mother Nature, weeping, stoops
to shed her tearstained kiss.
Cascading droplets one by one,
pierced on emerald blades,
A caressing hush with fondling fingers
Sooths the verdant glade.
Hooked on albescent lifeless limbs,
dreamlike whispering dew.
Life and death intertwined,
pleach-plash, a haunting hue.
Blinking beaded teardrops
Reflect the awakening sun,
lattice lacework, jewelled bedecked,
glinting, glistening, slung.
Shimmering, shivering, quivering trails,
criss-crossing gossamer threads,
Crippled outstretched hands awaiting, beauty baiting,
swallows up the dead.
Hidden dangers, who can tell,
what it is we find?
When we creep through ghostly cobwebs
in the corners of our mind.

GALLOPING TO MY GRAVE

The clouds pull their curtains and blank out the moon,
the dark grinds its teeth as it champs at the gloom.
Night's nails grate away at the bark of the day,
my destiny hides in the corner to play.

A stirrup has caught my flat foot in its grasp,
I'm nearing my death will this ride be my last?
I mount my grey mare, her breath bleeds in the night,
her nostrils blow bubbles of trouble and fright.

Pinned to my panic, red eyes throw their flames,
with spasms of terror, I pull on the reins.
Damnation is close as I tighten the slack,
are sins my companions? I cannot look back.

I have two black serpents they hang on each side,
and Satan's behind me, he came for the ride.

I AM A DAGLOCK[1]

An early morning cough gobs its phlegm, buffing the
      coarseness of the fields.
Warps and wefts weighty with mucus await the potential
      richness of the day.
Tousled storm clouds bounce across the mantle of
      your face.
Those curls, O those curls, that spring like lambs with wills
      of their own.

Eyes of absence, flat as a griddle, dark as drossy sheep dip,
torment from their troughs of ignorance.
Daggy I bleat, amongst the hills, for my bellwether beast,
lost in the foggy gauze of our panting breaths.

A chiselled boot scraper chin forged in iron,
juts from the shag of your mourning suit and mows
the razor-sharp blades that run nowhere and are endless.
I pad the field heavy as a finger that cannot filch.

Hanging around your hind leg I am no more, no less,
      than a daglock.
White flags surrender on ancient thorns, as faceless
      I follow the flock.

---

1   A daglock is a dung-caked lock of wool around the hindquarters
of a sheep

DIAMOND IN THE SKY

My
pointed
peaceful star,
appearing from afar.
Her shining tempting face,
how my beating heart, it raced.
My star-crossed lover appeared and left.
Piercing pain sad again, bereft.
Rough diamond knife spliced,
A weary wasted life,
In truth confess,
pointless.

ALONG THE BRUTAL SHORES OF MY WORLD

The shadowy ghosts of my former self stretch out
      from my feet,
Like tides of flat floundering dabs, along the cold
      solitary beach.
The grainy air swallows up the inaudible cursing of
      my misery.
The sap of suffering cork screws me into the
      curvaceous dunes.
My grunts and groans bubble and foam in the
      rip-rap of hurt,
Surfing my ulcered mouth like a salient sweet.
Memoires stain my mind with their oil polluting
      piercing ink.
Re-enactments of events are shaped in the currents of my
      spiralling drop.
Ocean-masters race up my spine pricking the corners of
      my consciousness.
Swirling and shunted in the tide's brainstorm of pain,
Like the driftwood's face pushed into the sand,
I spit out the grains of sadness and crawl towards the sea.
The battle of breathing the tempest becomes a chore.
No rescuing ethereal hand in the stinging shards of rain.
My eyes hurt seeing the vacancy the blackened flow
      of the sea.

I rise and fall like the determined waves screaming out to
the breaking of the day,
As I smash myself to pieces along the brittle shores of my
drowning world.

THE DARK SOUL

He, with a dark soul,
Feels the winter of despair,
Locked in his own cell.

I WILL NOT BE
WINDOW DRESSED

I will not be window dressed,
to impress.
My spirit calls,
I want to stand naked with all my flaws.
With head held high,
I'll stare you with my third bright eye.
Pretentious ones that make the noise,
You are not the peacemakers,
or contemplators, but agitators.
We all lie quietly when our time comes,
in immortal death, in graves lined one by one.
So don't tell me how to behave and what to say,
I will not be window dressed to impress.
My imperfections I'll wear, like stars in my hair,
and your opinions I don't really care.
Save me from my so called friends and foes,
My identity I'll wear as clothes. ·
The transformation is all to see,
My mind that served you now serves me.

ADDICTION

In the depths of my nicotine-stained room,
Only he and I exist,
Breathlessly speaking,
With glorious smoking tongues.
My phoenix rises from the ashes,
And scrawls big C's upon my ceiling.
I pay no heed to the warning,
Tattooed with tar on my wall,
"Smoking Kills".
His odorous breath next to mine,
Drowns my mind with cravings.
Wispy fingers fondle my clothes,
Filling my pockets with stale perfume.
Without a flicker of remorse,
He threatens to stub out my future.
My resistance fades,
Tangled sinews ignite,
And in my weakness,
I reach out for his tempting lips,
Yearning for the kiss of death.

I AM A MEMORIAL TO THE TORTURED SOUL

I am a memorial to the tortured soul,
lost in the grey stonework of an unforgiving parish,
I realize in the darkling hour l have barely loved at all.
An audience of spirits hover, awaiting my redemption.

Lost in the grey stonework of an unforgiving parish,
angels find me companionless, but I will not follow
    the light.
An audience of spirits hover, awaiting my redemption.
I wrestle with my unfaithfulness in the shadows of my sins.

Angels find me companionless, but I will not follow
    the light.
Of all the tracks I travelled, I struggled to find myself.
I wrestle with my unfaithfulness in the shadows of my sins,
as God speaks to deaf ears on this earth full of tears.

Of all the tracks I travelled, I struggled to find myself.
I am a memorial to the tortured soul.
As God speaks to deaf ears on this earth full of tears,
I realize in my darkest hour I have barely loved at all.

A LEAF IN THE CHAPTER
OF WAR

Upon the cold uncaring brow of winter,
When time with no meaning has silently splintered.
A shy, solitary, ragged dressed leaf,
Struggles amongst the gunshots of disbelief.

Down, down lady dances to death's dying beat,
As guns tap their feet, whilst souls left to weep.
Drawn to the gates of hell, void of all hope,
In the far side of despair lonely hands grope.

Spiralling, spinning, to greet gaunt ghosts of man,
Soaked in poppy red blood in faraway lands.
With a sad soul in the madness, she silently rests,
By the soiled sullied figure gasping for breath.

Trembling as one the leaf light as a feather,
Caresses his cheek as they both die together.

NIGHT'S TORMENT

In my night's torment,
The winter of discontent,
Creeps chillingly on.

POINTING TO NINE

There is no misery like the slow creeping of age
    in the unwinding of days.
Memories fade like the final tock of an echoing
    grandfather clock.
As the small ornate arthritic finger once again
    points to nine,
Forgetfulness devours my final hours in the clouding of
    my muddled mind.

Memories fade like the final tock of an echoing
    grandfather clock.
When minutes disappear in the creeping of death,
Forgetfulness devours my final hours in the clouding of
    my muddled mind,
And vacantly I stare into crannies of my room searching
    for my redemption.

When minutes disappear in the creeping of death,
Wearily I stumble along the frosty paths of my lost youth,
And vacantly I stare into crannies of my room searching
    for my redemption.
The bronzed pendulum swings like the sagging skin
    around my aching bones.

Wearily I stumble along the frosty paths of my lost youth.
There is no misery like the slow creeping of age in the
unwinding of days,
The bronzed pendulum swings like the sagging skin
around my aching bones,
As the small ornate arthritic finger once again
points to nine.

LIFE IN THE SHADOW OF DEATH

In loneliness, can I cope, left only with the frayed
    constituency of my thoughts?
Death clawed at our door, and with a trembling of fear,
    my husband summoned it in.
Only time with its tears tried to tell, what I couldn't face,
    but my heart knew well.
I stared grief in the eye, and with its bleak stain of winter
    it stared back.

Death clawed at our door, and with a trembling of fear,
    my husband summoned it in.
Anger kept me connected to life as I spun on my axis
    of pain.
I stared grief in the eye, and with its bleak stain of winter
    it stared back.
My soul was splintered with sorrow, eyeing the hunger
    of his cancer.

Anger kept me connected to life as I spun on my axis
of pain.
My husband's longanimity showed great strength,
but alas he weakened.
My soul was splintered with sorrow, eyeing the hunger
of his Cancer.
Life's directions disappeared along the predetermined
tracks of my fate.

My husband's longanimity showed great strength,
but alas he weakened.
In loneliness, can I cope, left only with the frayed
constituency of my thoughts?
Life's directions disappeared along the predetermined
tracks of my fate.
Only time with its tears tried to tell, what I couldn't face,
but my heart knew well.

MY FATHER

He was the fading of the day,
he was the echo far away.
No blinking of the dusty eye,
a vacant stare in a greying sky.

He was not deep like oceans wide,
we lived in the shallows of the tide.
He was the dent-de-lion clock,
he was the disappearing sock.

Skin deep pockets love slipped through,
his tightness was a new school shoe.
Soft hugs a fingertip away,
were lost in brief wafts of decay.

A hoary crown cropped so severe,
his whistling aid ate up his ear.
A bulbous nose sorrowed his face,
his hollow grin slid out of place.

Clothes in boredom shone with age,
his jacket bland in biscuit beige.
A lonely voice that no one heard,
No pity for the dying bird.

Two sugars in his cup of tea,
I didn't know him, he didn't know me.

BEIGE JACKETS

Beige jackets. Beige jackets everywhere. Essential clothing as you rapidly decline into old age. My father cherished one, so worn, so shabby it could have walked away on its own. Polyester, it has to be polyester. Devoid of any style, resting just below the waist. Straight up, straight down, a vision of lollipop sticks with silver crowns.

The grey brigade continually struggle up and down High Streets in their compulsory uniforms. Sometimes somebody breaks rank and wears an identical jacket but silver grey. Sticks, zimmer frames, disability scooters all kitted out the same with beige jacket frail companions shuffling around in the mimicry of life. Camouflaged within the nondescript background of life, the dying melt away, never to be remembered.

I am an old aged pensioner, but give me scarlet jeans and crippling sparkly shoes in any colour bright, with highest heels and styles so chic that clitter clatter down the street.

People may laugh at my rainbow colours and people may stare. Colour is the vibrancy of life, why would I care?

When life is through and I cannot hack it, please don't leave me at the heavenly gates swaddled in a beige jacket.

AGED MOLE

Perplexed in a coal black room of loneliness,
turning pale with indifference, shuffling.
A squeezing of my wheezing lungs,
lost consonants, vowels, muddled in the muffling.
Approaching with apprehension tangled roots,
of Heaven, or is it Hell?
I fought from my hills with loud opinions,
now coffined in my defence I dwell.
A prisoner hopelessly wandering,
through darkened tunnels of accelerated time.
Stonkered I spade in my blindness,
around twisted truths in a wavering line.

TUMOURS

The excrescences appeared upon his body, and day by day he realised he had to chase his dreams away. The exuberance of his life had to be redacted. He visited the specialist with a fusillade of questions of which there were no answers. Each day he persevered with his treatment. Life whorled out of control. The pressures of the crises were weighty. BUT …

In his quiet space,
He gave himself permission,
To hope for the best.

THE SILENT TEAR

With outstretched hands I touch the fear,
my fractured heart's shattered in two,
the saddest is the silent tear.

A smog of pain hangs low, won't clear,
I trawl the mist, but where are you?
With outstretched hands I touch the fear.

My future's grey ash blows so near,
I need your arms, what can I do?
the saddest is the silent tear.

The landscape of your smile appears,
I cannot face the final truth,
with outstretched hands I touch the fear.

My calling fell upon deaf ears,
I thought we were the chosen few,
the saddest is the silent tear.

My wanting rides the night that jeers,
despair's an arch my life twists through.
With outstretched hands I touch the fear,
the saddest is the silent tear.

THE TORMENTED TOAD

Squashed I squat amongst the feculent swamps of
    my own making,
Like a pustule waiting to burst forth upon the
    wetness of earth's wounds.
Mantled in mists, like steam in a tagine, remote
    from happy,
I stare swollen-eyed into night's blindness waiting
    for morning's misplaced light.

My croaks wander loud and deep as they travel in
    the direction of my fears,
And roll down the echoing corridors of my future's
    eternal emptiness.
With thoughts sealed inwards, my heart openly
    pulsates outside of itself.
Bloated, like a greedy man's distended belly, I await
    your pardon.

The rain cracks the dull mirrors of the marshes,
    exposing the truth.
Swaddled in reeds taut and tall, where death creeps,
    I utter 'Please love me, warts and all.'

THE RELUCTANT JOURNEY

I glance sideways and watch his lids like silk Austrian blinds fold gently down over his eyes, snuffing out the starkness of day.

"What are you staring at?" he snaps.

"Nothing, nothing" I reply, letting my words swallow up the air.

"Just checking you are OK."

He tosses me one of his harsh huffs that frequently arrive stamping at my door. I fix my eyes on the bulbous black backside of a Chelsea tractor ahead of me which probably has bull bars on the front. Maybe there is a herd of wildebeest roaming across the plains of the A38? I stare in my husband's direction again and catch a glimpse of a lone ray of sunshine skipping over his brindled yellowing parchment skin.

"What would you like to eat tonight? Your wish is my command," I chirrup like a hopeful genie desperate to obey.

"I don't know," he sighs despondently.

"Surprise me, but nothing too salty," he demands.

I know immediately that whatever I put in front of him he probably won't eat it. My thoughts play hop scotch between fish and chips and quiche. I wonder what the fox will want today? He seems to be the only one who hungrily eats the food I cook. I plead in silence for a swift answer from my husband, but his mouth remains dry with the grit of despondency.

We travel on at a snail's pace stopping and starting whilst ensnared in the winding grimy entrails of the traffic. The grey sky hovers above the day bringing with it a swathe of depression. Suddenly, without warning a car horn calls out from behind. Startled Ian awakes suddenly from the fog of his sleep and booms out:

"What the hell?"

"It's alright I think the idiot behind reckons I'm in the wrong lane and I'm not," I tell him, my lips disappearing into the bars of my teeth.

Ian swivels around to give the driver inappropriate finger gestures. This is not the Ian I have known and loved. Who is this man? He was always so placid and gentle, but now he reacts to the worsening thoughts gathering en-masse in his head. I accommodate his mood swings knowing I have to view the difficulties of our lives from another platform.

My mind wanders to the sunny side of my brain to when we were young. What a big, handsome man Ian was. My rock, my fella. I felt so safe in his arms, but now the years have taken their toll. His strength has disappeared into a long dark passage and weakness has busied itself in its place. I search his face for the kindness of time, and see only the barren tracks of fate. I look across at him with my watchful gaze and see him withering like un un-watered plant in his seat. We couple again for a brief moment amongst the harshness of reality.

"Have you got all that you need?"

"Yes, yes," he replies.

"Only checking."

As a loving gesture, I stretch out my hand and finger his bony knee. He refuses to acknowledge it and swiftly moves his leg away, lost in the darkness of his own space. Although frail, I know he is still his own master and watch him holding on tightly to his inner self. I find myself alone once again, lost in the thicket of my own selfish thinking.

"Maybe when we've finished what we have to do, we go somewhere and have a cup of coffee?" I enquire.

He wearily responds with a reply dipped in anger. "All we do now is huddle in coffee shops and drown our sorrows in mugs of Chai latte. I'm sick of it all."

I duck his barbed words. He is not travelling to a good place and I am reluctantly following. I understand that everyone is allowed the freedom to express themselves, and even offend their loved ones with the roughness of their bark, so I do not respond to his drugged filled words and continue instead to listen to the busy hum of traffic and with a vice like grip strangle the steering wheel. I keep the frayed edges of me tucked up tightly. It serves no purpose to let myself unravel in front of him. I watch his head sink into his shoulders like a replaced cork squashed in the top of a wine bottle and for a few minutes we bathe in the silence of the moment.

We proceed on our journey locked in the fog of pessimism until we reach our destination. I swing my Crimson Citroen into the greyness of the car park. Ian leans forward and groaning scoops up his paperwork from the floor. I grab at his hand and squeeze it tightly. Ian expels a thoughtful breath that floats above his solemn head.

"I really don't want to be here again, I really don't."

"I know my love," I say compassionately. "But what choice to we have? I can't lose you."

My mind wanders to our wedding day all those distant years ago. I recall our vows "In sickness and in health." How I skipped and danced over the words at nineteen years of age, not realising the true extent of their meaning.

"It's soon our 50th wedding anniversary and you aren't going anywhere without me, anyway I want my gold locket."

He tosses me the twisted pickings of his smile. "Don't worry my darling you will have it even if it kills me, which it probably will."

We chuckle together in a lighter mood which comes to greet us through the blankness of the day.

"I really don't want this chemo again," he says stretching out his words like a plate in the hands of a beggar.

"But you have to my darling, what choice do you have," I reply with leaking eyes and words bordering on terror.

We grasp at one another, and rejoice again that I have found him and he has found me.

LIFE IS ONLY SLEEPING

In the cold pitiless attrition, the fluttering of snow
    silently drifts.
Angel feathers softly fall, laying their pristine pinions
    upon the frozen earth.
Chalky flakes, tortured to death, are penned by my
    gloved hand, LIFE IS ONLY SLEEPING.
I stand in the bleak tenebrous day, shivering in the glass
    iced whispering breath.

Angel feathers softly fall, laying their pristine pinions
    upon the frozen earth,
Blanketing my lonely footprints, stamped amongst the
    ruins of winter.
I stand in the bleak tenebrous day, shivering in the glass
    iced whispering breath.
Befuddled cobwebs trail from dead limbs and defiant
    red-bloodied berries.

Blanketing my lonely footprints, stamped amongst the
    ruins of winter,
The mantle of the earth lies still and buried within its
    frozen tomb.
Befuddled cobwebs trail from dead limbs and defiant
    red-bloodied berries.
The tyranny of frost is apparent as the blank pages of the
    fields lie wordless.

The mantle of the earth lies still and buried within its
      frozen tomb.
In the cold pitiless attrition, the fluttering of snow
      silently drifts.
The tyranny of frost is apparent as the blank pages of
      the fields lie wordless.
Chalky flakes, tortured to death, are penned by my
      gloved hand, LIFE IS ONLY SLEEPING.

PERSEID

From illuminating motes my meteor man sprang,
To lighten this stargazer's chain of darkness.
My eyes looked upwards but remained dimmed,
Until my universe became you, and only you.
Indignations of frost, were lost,
In the sprinkling snow of hope,
From his unspoken words.
The dimension of my soul shone bright,
Then grew thin, with the sudden passing
Of the revelations of his sins.
The shimmering crystal ice,
Grew thicker within his brittle heart.
In pretence I dusted over the cracks,
Of my mounting consternations.
I laid low beneath the luminous constellation.
The transference of my reflective love,
Shimmered high, but did not warm the night's sky.
I climbed, contemplative in my mind's eye,
to the outer reaches of the Heavens.
You fired your arrows bright,
Across the boughs of my passion.
With your coldness and insensitivity,
You snuffed me out.

Sanity was swiftly spent,
No longer to vent my emotions,
You showered me with permeating stars of kisses,
No flashing hits but swift the misses.
As quickly as you came you left.
Bereft I watched my meteor man,
Vanish into the shadows of the night.

GRANDCHILDREN

Sweet like the plumpness of the drop,
That flops upon the mirrored puddle pot.
You are the flush of the shying blush,
The peeking snowdrops in winter's dust.
The feathery kiss of an angel's wing,
The coloured swirls of a rainbow ring.
You are the clatter of the chatter,
The sweetest giggling of the laughter.
The tip toe footprints upon my heart,
The moon bright beams dancing in the dark.
The ping and pong of a bouncing ball,
The happiness flowers in a garden wall.
The tears of joy fill my eyes,
You are the sunbeams warming my skies.

ONE LITTLE BIRD

Faltering in the darkness she winged, keeping her back
    to the rain.
A feathered fledgling stained by untruths taught herself
    how to survive,
And trilled sweetly with shrill notes of joy,
    in her softening of pain,
As she struggled to survive in the harshness of the world.

A feathered fledgling stained by untruths taught herself
    how to survive.
Thrown from the comfort of her nest,
    into the chaos dropped.
As she struggled to survive in the harshness of the world,
One little bird in her premature weakness,
    winged her way in life.

Thrown from the comfort of her nest,
    into the chaos dropped.
Damaged by the frosty burns of her parents' genes,
One little bird in her premature weakness,
    winged her way in life,
And flew through the greyness of the sky,
    with emotions eggshell thin.

Damaged by the frosty burns of her parents' genes,
Faltering in the darkness she winged,
    keeping her back to the rain,
And flew through the greyness of the sky,
    with emotions eggshell thin,
And trilled sweetly with shrill notes of joy,
    in her softening of pain.

IN THE SHALLOWS OF MY SOUL

Not too deep I creep,
Where iridescent blue shoals,
Of past lovers, swim by,
In my thought filled clouds.

Hung are haunting memories,
Of their fast, fading faces,
High, out of reach,
In the misty skies gallery of echoes.

I study their features,
Which gradually dissipate,
Into the ether,
Of my own self-doubt.

Menacing phantoms,
Of my sinfulness, reappear.
And in the darkness of my world,
I lay justice to my lonely life.

In my ambitious mind,
I await with fever, a new coming.
My soulmate, my comforter,
I seek you out in the storm clouds gathering.

Will you remain?
To kindle this frigid soul's flame.
Digging down deep,
I search out an empathy.

With the defeated,
I say farewell,
To my tranquil mind.
Where pretence was my only friend.

Return me to the safety of the past.
Let me tumble backwards,
Back into the tedium of time,
Where all remained normal.

The slow pace of boredom kept me sane.
It was a time where I could swim on my back,
And freely paddle, without thought,
In the shallows of my soul.

UNANSWERABLE TEARS

Ethereal memories in autumnal mists,
Slow their deathly pace,
As sharp winter blades cut my flesh,
I try to recall his heavenly face.
I moisten his ghostly grave with tears,
Falling like blinding rain.
Cloaked in misery I sob,
In the summit of my pain.
With my heart as a hunter,
I wonder aloud, about my destiny.
Wanton starved lips,
No more to be kissed,
A premonition of what will be?
A wind mocks the fleeting of the day,
And laughs at death through dying leaves,
Which dissipate in the worthless shadows,
And the wretchedness that winter heaves.
In my loneliness, who do I cry for?
Pray my guides, tell me who?
For a love cut short in sorrowful times,
Or do I selfishly sob for myself,
And not you?

LONELY FOOTPRINTS

Silent flow my tears,
Lonely footprints lead to me,
In the blanket snow.

DEBASED DREAMS

Daily dreams debased,
Trapped in the stresses of life.
Makes one feel useless.

JAPANESE KOI

Who coloured the rainbow? Who brocaded the
      Japanese Koi?
Foraging forms layered so thick, shimmer in the
      lap of light.
Lost forever in transitory dreams, shapes softly
      swim in endless circles.
Who needs persuasion to lower their eyes and see
      such majesty.

Foraging forms layered so thick, shimmer in the
      lap of light.
Quizzical below the ambiguous shadows of the skies,
      their thoughts are shaped.
Who needs persuasion to lower their eyes and see
      such majesty?
Opening and shutting pursed lips, like whispers in
      the wind, silently call to us.

Quizzical below the ambiguous shadows of the skies,
      their thoughts are shaped.
Mouths shoot out a radiance of unspoken words
      that speak no guile.
Opening and shutting pursed lips, like whispers in
      the wind, silently call to us.
In the depths of our wandering minds, between the
      balance of time.

Mouths shoot out a radiance of unspoken words,
that speak no guile.
Who coloured the rainbow? Who brocaded the
Japanese Koi?
In the depths of our wandering minds, between
the balance of time,
Lost forever in transitory dreams, shapes softly
swim in endless circles.

PEACE AND JOY

GOLD, Frankincense and myrrh, precious gifts,
Moon mellow peeping from spidery web mist.
Silver bells call to the shining star,
Weary guests travelling from afar,
The argent beacon hauntingly brings.
Over frost dipped hills in amity, carols ring.

Spellbound children search the skies,
Illusions of sleighs in their watchful eyes.
Nestling presents hug the tree,
Loving gifts to you from me.
Gleaming dust interspersed whips the pallid earth,
Virgin winged, sweet angels sing, heralding Jesus' birth.

In the final hours of manic pace,
And the last till tings and lunacy fades.
Mother Nature her pallid cloak slings,
Wrapping with love the last bird on the wing.
In twilight, her powdered sparkling beauty shines,
Flawless from rabid footprints, in passage of time.

Doily flakes flick grasslands dying blades,
And on the frozen fencing lays.
Gnarled ghostly limbs tap ashen keys,
With icy fingers on the breeze.
Peace, joy and solace amongst soothing trees,
Search your soul in silence, and in the stillness BE.

I HEARD YOU SOFTLY CALL MY NAME

Somewhere deep within my pitiless shroud of sorrow,
In the wilderness between life and death's rushing winds,
I heard you softly call my name,
Whilst loping phantoms walked the night,
    ambushing my thoughts.

In the wilderness between life and death's rushing winds.
I grasped your refreshing rain of words to cleanse
    my prejudices.
Whilst loping phantoms walked the night,
    ambushing my thoughts,
Heaven's gate flung open and shone its silvery light.

I grasped at your refreshing rain of words, to cleanse
    my prejudices.
Upon the draconian darkness that draped my soul,
Heaven's gate flung open and shone its silvery light,
As the air sighed and mellowed to your mellifluous tones.

Upon the draconian darkness that draped my soul,
Somewhere deep within my pitiless shroud of sorrow.
As the air sighed and mellowed to your mellifluous tones,
I heard you softly call my name.

SCARLET SENTRY

Heaving heart with breast so red,
He's standing guard with slanted head.
Front and back with nervous twitch,
Stamping up and down his pitch.

Back and forth sharp eagle eyed,
Spots intruders from the skies.
The sentry hops along his base,
Daring them to show their face.

All along the watch tower stands,
Showing them that he is grand.
Rifled wings, fine feathers bright,
He won't give up, without a fight.

Within his territory, food he guards,
Blocks of seeds and nuts and lard.
Chirruping he dares them all,
The little soldier's marching tall.

Always first to greet the dawn,
On every frosty frigid morn.
He chirrups loud and oh so sweet,
The echoes bounce along the street.

With sweetest face, and coat so grand,
I watch my Robin take his stand.

SEASCAPE

Diminishing carmine greets the smalt seam of
man's mystery.

An ebbing force sketches sweeping curvatures on
its coffee canvas.

Dotted ants scurry to and forth sulking branded wooden
hulks, fingers poised upwards, on the contours of the
scene. Each sinister shape adorns a secret cloak. Scrawled
warps and wefts. Lines caressing lines.

Secret sable abstractions quiver in the lapse. Leaded peace,
time trapped, reflects in the briny wrinkles of hesitant
ocean veins. Transmitted gems kiss each frown, twinkling
beneath the irrigator. The sinking sun. Sacred verdure and
umber adjacent strokes of forgotten blistered vegetation
highlights sparse sections of cloth.

Am I an imposer on a masterpiece, impressing life on a
picture? Coupled with the occasional screeching scavenger
scanning for outcasts pulsating in the veins, I tread
stealthily so not to scratch the canvas.

Such artistry. Can I but paint within you reflected images?
Created coastline. A painting named *Seascape*.

The artist is God.

THE WEATHER OF
THE HEART

In the unpredictable weather of the heart,
In the cold pitiless attrition,
A fluttering of memories silently drift.
Angels lay their snowy pinions,
Upon the unforgiving earth,
Of my mind,
To ease the insuperable pain.
Trapped in the bleak tenebrous days,
Of my deep midwinter, I shiver.
The rush of short days,
Catches my breath.
And in the ruins,
And the ticking tides of time,
I search for a release,
Amongst the cold strange light.
On the blank white pages,
Of frozen fields,
My lonely footprints,
Maybe spell out my fate.
The pages of my future,
Before me lay wordless.
The tyranny of frost,
Is apparent in my face.
I hold out my hand,

For the bud that must appear,
In the lap of spring's light.
I await the stretched-out days,
And the soft kisses of the sun.
I await in anticipation,
A new beginning,
A new love.
In winter's bleakness,
Wrapped up in a scarf of himself,
My malapert man departs,
Along with the old year.

THE LONELY TOAD

Bulbous eyed I croaked,
Amongst the lonely shadows,
The dark silence spoke.

WHO OVERFILLED
MY BUCKET?

Who overfilled my bucket?
With flea coloured puce,
Of pugnacious juice.
Who overfilled my bucket?

Who overfilled my bucket?
With, a bubbling foaming floss,
Of egotistical tear-stained dross.
Who overfilled my bucket?

Who overfilled my bucket?
With waves of greed that rock the tin,
My hopes as rusty as the rim.
Who overfilled my bucket?

Who overfilled my bucket?
There is a tiny festering hole,
Dripping segments of my dying soul.
Who overfilled my bucket?

Who overfilled my bucket?
Hope in the mullock of my mind,
In heaviness is treading time.
Who overfilled my bucket?

Who overfilled my bucket?
My childhood was so stained with pain,
My mind it really needs to change.
Who overfilled my bucket?

Who overfilled my bucket?
It's filled to the brim with past decay,
There's nothing more for me to say.
Who overfilled my bucket?

Who overfilled my bucket?
It's me, Oh F—K IT!

A WANDERING ROAD

Outside a gold dipped sun attempts to smile between the
    clusters of cloud scudding its face.
I hesitate to open myself to a world of madness to let the
    future in, fearing what I may see.
A wandering road beckons, and bestows a faint trail of
    hope upon my apathy.
Losing direction, this seasoned traveller pauses by a river of
    thoughts, pursuing her identity.

I hesitate to open myself to a world of madness to let the
    future in, fearing what I may see.
I realize with a fake smile I will soon have to walk another
    lonely path that invites my tread.
Losing direction, this seasoned traveller pauses by a river of
    thoughts, pursuing her identity.
Memories like autumn leaves blow across my path, seeking
    refuge in their own dark space.

I realize with a fake smile I will soon have to walk another
    lonely path that invites my tread.
Curses and consequences knock on my door, binding me
    to the empty solace of my room.
Memories like autumn leaves blow across my path, seeking
    refuge in their own dark space.
With a broth of doubts, I trek through my solitary griefs
    that lead nowhere and are endless.

Curses and consequences knock on my door, binding me
      to the empty solace of my room.
Outside a gold dipped sun attempts to smile between the
      clusters of cloud scudding its face.
With a broth of doubts, I trek through my solitary griefs
      that lead nowhere and are endless.
A wandering road beckons and bestows a faint trail of hope
      upon my apathy.

THE COTSWOLDS

A raptor with dark intentions circles the blue axle of
    Heaven, and dives upon the Cotswolds.
The morning rays thatch the verdant blades and wild
    flowers that run nowhere in particular,
As a soft speaking breeze nets my breath, and blows its
    gentle kisses on my wanton lips.
I climb up, not back, through sunshine rapeseed, which
    purges my mind with tranquillity.

The morning rays thatch the verdant blades and wild
    flowers that run nowhere in particular.
Comforting homes of buttered stone lay strewn amongst
    the undulations of my world.
I climb up, not back, through sunshine rapeseed, which
    purges my mind with tranquillity.
Life's dawn ignites the earth's mantle and places her healing
    hand upon my fretful brow.

Comforting homes of buttered stone lay strewn amongst
    the undulations of my world.
An echo of a birthing cow runs amok through the silence
    of the hills and takes possession.
Life's dawn ignites the earth's mantle and places her healing
    hand upon my fretful brow.
Churches weep with unanswered questions nailed on
    crosses, memorials to vanishing faces.

An echo of a birthing cow runs amok through the silence
of the hills and takes possession.
A raptor with dark intentions circles the blue axle of
Heaven, and dives upon the Cotswolds.
Churches weep with unanswered questions nailed on
crosses, memorials to vanishing faces,
As a soft speaking breeze nets my breath, and blows its
gentle kisses on my wanton lips.